Love and Hate

Mary Love Dance

authorHOUSE®

AuthorHouse™
1663 Liberty Drive
Bloomington, IN 47403
www.authorhouse.com
Phone: 833-262-8899

Published by AuthorHouse 02/16/2021

ISBN: 978-1-5246-7132-7 (sc)
ISBN: 978-1-5246-7130-3 (hc)
ISBN: 978-1-5246-7131-0 (e)

Library of Congress Control Number: 2017916072

This book is dedicated to my family whom has shown me the true meaning of love and the struggles families have around loving one another. Love is complicated and beautiful. The old adage there is a thin line between love and hate is true. I hope you find these poems comforting, enlightening and it makes you think about the love you share and experience each day.

"The best and most beautiful things in this world cannot be seen or even heard, but must be felt with the heart."

- Helen Keller

Contents

Love

What is There But Love? 1
Love Me 3
And The Greatest of These is Love 5
Love you! 7
What is Love? 9
You Complete My Life 11
My Pledge to You 13
Without Love 15
Will You Feel That Way Forever 17
What is Old is New Again 19

Dying Love

My Dying Heart 23
Love? 25
What Do You Want? 27
Your Twisted Love 29
I Long for Attention 31
What's the Cost of Your Love? 33
Trains Passing in the Night 35
Are You Waiting for Me Too 37
How Can I Conquer Your Love 39
How Can I Change You 41

Suppressive Love

Love 45

Your Love is Like a Flower 47

When You Love Someone 49

You Live and Hope to Find 51

Just One Day 53

Look at Me 55

Falling 57

The Cost of Your Love 59

Hate

I Hate You 63

Hate is on Your Shoulders 65

I Hear You Cry 67

Why I Hate Your Love 69

Seductive Love

When You Say You Love Me 73

Passion 75

Your Queen 77

My Love is Exponential 79

When Love Takes Hold of You 81

The One Has Become Two 83

Convenient Love 85

I feel Something 87

My Spirit is Touched 89

Morning, Noon or Night 91

A Touch Unknown Seems 93

Love

"Love is experienced from the beginning of life, a look, a feeling, a smile or a warm touch. We all need it and denial of it causes instability, low self-esteem and hardship." - Mary Love Dance

Discussion Questions

1. Think about your first awareness of love. What emotions do you can recall as you remember that love?

_____
_____
_____
_____
_____
_____
_____

2. How do your emotions then compare with your feeling about, and understanding of love now?

_____
_____
_____
_____
_____
_____
_____

3. How would the world change if you consciously gave more love?

_____
_____
_____
_____
_____
_____
_____

4. What problems would we resolve if we really truly loved our neighbor?

_____
_____
_____
_____
_____
_____
_____

What is There But Love?

What is there but
Love
to hold on to
and believe in

What is there but
Love
to take you
through the day

What is there but
Love
the answer for
your behaviors

What is there but
Love
while God will
give you favor

What is there but
Love
the backbone
of elation

What is there but
Love
we'd be
a better nation

What is there but
Love
to spread to
All Mankind

What is there but
Love
it only takes
being kind

What is there but
Love
to give
to another

What is there but
Love
we all came from
one mother

Love Me

Love me
be proud of me
praise me like a fine car
Love me
be proud of me
that will take you far

Have compassion for me
admire me
for all that I am
Have compassion for me
admire me
every single strain

Comfort me
and build me up
never put me down
Comfort me
build me up
and always be around

Why, because
I love you, Man

Discussion Questions

1. What impact does pride have on how you love someone?

_____

_____

2. How does someone else's compassion and love help lift you up?

_____

_____

3. Does the way your spouse supports/lifts you up affect other relationships you have?

_____

_____

4. Think about a time someone has supported you, what impact did their support have on you?

_____

_____

Love Never Ends. It's amazing how you can give it and never run out of the ability to give it.
5. Can true love serve as a constant protection for you?

_____

_____

6. Can love be self-seeking?

_____

_____

7. Does or should the person who loves you always have the strength to give you what you need?

_____

_____

8. How do you find someone who gives you love that will guard and protect you?

_____

_____

9. Why is finding love that will protect you important to a lasting relationship?

_____

_____

And The Greatest of These is Love...

Love is patient and love is kind
If you love someone keep this in mind

It does not boast, and not so proud
So don't brag when in a crowd

It does not dishonor nor is it self-seeking
But holds your heart close for constant safe keeping

It's not easily angered and keeps no record of wrong
It reminds you of the ballad of a sweet, sweet love song

Love does not delight in evil acts
So there will never be "The Big Pay Back"

It rejoices in truth
and guards you too
That's what loving's
suppose to do

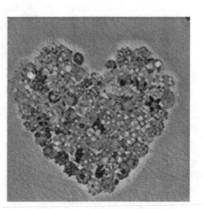

It always Protects
Trusts
Hopes
and Perseveres
It stays around
and keeps love in Reserve

It never fails
so there's your plan
The best advice
in all the land

And if you abide in these each day
You'll create a honored and brighter way
For all who follow God's plan
Their Love and Marriage
Will Forever Stand

Discussion Questions

1. Are you now or have you ever been in love?

_____

_____

_____

_____

_____

_____

_____

2. How does loving yourself affect your capacity to love someone else?

_____

_____

_____

_____

_____

_____

3. How do we learn how to love others?

_____

_____

_____

_____

_____

_____

4. Do you believe that human touch alone can express love?

_____

_____

_____

_____

_____

_____

Love you!

Why is it
when I talk to you
I feel something
special

Why is it
when I'm by your side
I don't want to go
away

Why is it
just the sound of your voice
makes me
want to stay

Why is it
when we are
no longer
talking
that I can truly smile

Why is it
when I think
of you
you make my
soul go wild

Why is it
that I have
a funny feeling
every time
you're on
my mind

Why is it
that you
bring me
so much joy
I can't
contain
My Heart

I
hope
this will
Never Go
Away
and
Always
Survives
Each day

You make me smile!

What is Love?

What is love
can it be defined
how deep does it flow
is it ever a crime

What is love
the sky is the limit
how much can you give
and what's contained in it

What is love
how do you know
that you have true love
or is it a show

What is love
why do some people say
there's a thin line
between love & hate today

What is love
how can it glow
and why do we believe
it must continue to grow

Discussion Questions

1. Can love be a crime?

_____

_____

2. What, do you think motivates some people to kill in the name of love?

_____

_____

3. Can love be vast?

_____

_____

4. What does the vastness of love mean to you?

_____

_____

5. Do you feel another person can complete your life?

_____

_____

6. What are the benefits of not depending on anyone else in order to be complete?

_____

_____

7. Do you believe in destiny? Why or Why not?

_____

_____

8. Do you believe in a soulmate?

_____

_____

9. What are the top 5 characteristic you want your partner to have?

_____

_____

You Complete My Life

You complete my life
you satisfy my appetite
you are the sunshine of my life
and you make everything in my world right

You run my world
and I'm your favorite girl
you are the air that I breath
and you make my world swirl

You quench my thirst
I feel like I'm about to burst
you are my life and it's complete
and I'm so grateful God let us meet

You fulfill my daily needs
and I don't have to ever plead
for you are my everything
and you make me want to produce and sing

you are the reason that I live
you make me want to give and give
you get me and that's the real, real deal
you create in me a joy only you can fill

I never want to have this end
My joy and love is blowing in the wind
You keep me wanting more and more
and for this I truly adore...you

Discussion Questions

1. Besides a loving relationship, in what other circumstances might you pledge yourself?

_____

_____

_____

_____

_____

2. Do you think it is important to pledge (or give) your life to your mate?

_____

_____

_____

_____

_____

3. How can you make and keep your pledge?

_____

_____

_____

_____

_____

4. Will a pledge prolong your relationship?

_____

_____

_____

_____

_____

5. Would you die to protect your mate?

_____

_____

_____

_____

_____

My Pledge to You

I pledge my love to you
We are one in body
I give my all can you hear the thunder
Let no man ever put us under

I will
Respect you
Love you
Sacrifice for you
Adore you
Restore you
Support you
Add to you
Heighten Your Being

I pledge my love to you
I promise to give you my All
I will listen to your request
And never let you Fall

I will not
Disrespect you
Hate you
Envy you
Embarrass you
Take from you
Resent you

Whenever you need me
Till death do us part
I promise to compliment you
And give you my heart

Discussion Questions

1. Could we survive without love?
Do you think love holds the world together? Explain.

_____
_____
_____
_____
_____
_____
_____
_____
_____
_____
_____
_____
_____
_____
_____
_____

2. How can you contribute your love to humankind?

_____
_____
_____
_____
_____
_____
_____
_____
_____
_____
_____
_____
_____
_____
_____
_____

Without Love

Without love where would we be
it's very easy and we can see
that love is here for you and me
without love who would set you free

Without love there would be no joy
for every little girl and boy
this precious gift we cannot see
and that doesn't grow on a giving tree

Without love there would be great pain
from all the world's desires and gains
the joy of love we'd never reap
and we would not be able to keep

Without love hate would be the norm
and we would die in the mighty storm
but we are blessed to be able to have and give
and never run out of love as long as we live

Give Love

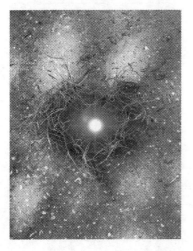

Discussion Questions

1. Do you believe that life can alter or change your love for someone?
Explain.

_____

_____

_____

_____

_____

_____

_____

_____

_____

2. Can you truly commit to someone for life?

_____

_____

_____

_____

_____

_____

_____

_____

_____

3. What do you have to do before you can make a commitment to someone
else for life?

_____

_____

_____

_____

_____

_____

_____

_____

_____

Will You Feel That Way Forever

On our wedding day
we took our vows
and made a commitment
to love one another and Wow
'till death do us part

On our wedding day before family
with God by our side
we made a commitment
to forever love
to our Savior above
'till death do us part

On our special day
as we gazed into each others eyes
and sealed our love
to honor one another
confident in our commitment
'till death do us part

On our wedding day
we believed it would last
and cast out all doubt in the past
and never again to challenge or disbelieve
That our true love would not excel and achieve

What is Old is New Again

Time can't erase the love we share
It always there floating in the air
When we feel low
and life has got us down
We cling to the fact
that our love will always be around

Time can't erase the pride we share
It's evident in moments and how we care
When we are challenged
and feel we can't go on
We are secure in the knowledge
that our love is strong

Time can't erase the joy we share
It's present in the good times and
laughs in the air
When obstacles get in the way
through faith and confidence
We find a new day

Time can't erase our bond
It's blessed by the most high and Holy One
We pray that you too someday will find
A love as pure and special as mine
Believe and it will come true
That what is old will also be new

Discussion Questions

1. As time goes by, how can you keep your love for your partner new?

_____

_____

_____

_____

_____

_____

2. How does love evolve with time? Explain.

_____

_____

_____

_____

_____

_____

3. What advice would you give a young couple to achieve lasting love?

_____

_____

_____

_____

_____

_____

4. Can you give advice to a couple if you have not maintained a relationship yourself?

_____

_____

_____

_____

_____

_____

Dying Love

"Be careful of a love that will kill your love. It wants to destroy, it longs to destroy you from the inside out." - Mary Love Dance

Discussion Questions

1. Can love kill love?

_____
_____
_____
_____
_____
_____
_____

2. If not, then why do people kill in the name of love?

_____
_____
_____
_____
_____
_____
_____

3. Is it possible to love and hate someone at the same time?

_____
_____
_____
_____
_____
_____
_____

4. In a love relationship can someone cause your love to die? Who is it responsible to shield and protect the love in a relationship?

_____
_____
_____
_____
_____
_____

My Dying Heart

Just like a dying flower
its pedals fall away
The leaves they dry and wither
and soon it will decay
The life is sucked right from it
like my cold and dying heart
I'm sad again, guess what you win
I want us to depart

Just like a dying flower
Our love there is no cure
There is no medication
and baby that's for sure
The time has come to say goodbye
and thus release the pain
To set you free away from me
New love, I'm sure you'll gain.

Discussion Questions

1. Is it a mistake to want someone to treat you like they treat themselves?

_____

_____

_____

_____

_____

_____

_____

_____

_____

_____

_____

_____

_____

_____

_____

2. Is there a way to foster the treatment you want from others?

_____

_____

_____

_____

_____

_____

_____

_____

_____

_____

_____

_____

_____

_____

Love?

Can you treat me
like you
treat
yourself
or do you realize?

Can you treat me
like you
treat
yourself
the apple of your eyes?

Can you treat me
like you
treat
yourself
the queen
I'm
meant to be?

Can you treat me
like you
treat
yourself
or wont you set me free?

Discussion Questions

1. What kind of love do you want and need?

_____
_____
_____
_____
_____
_____
_____
_____
_____
_____
_____
_____
_____
_____
_____
_____

2. Are you willing to give the love you want and need to your partner?

_____
_____
_____
_____
_____
_____
_____
_____
_____
_____
_____
_____
_____
_____
_____
_____

What Do You Want?

What do you want
Love
Why do you want
Love
What do you need
Love
Why do you need
Love
Why don't you give
Love
Why don't you have
Love
Why don't you show
Love
Why don't you grow
Love

Discussion Questions

1. Do you believe that true love can be twisted?

_____
_____
_____
_____
_____
_____
_____
_____
_____
_____
_____
_____
_____
_____
_____
_____
_____

2. Why do people say, "If I can't have you no one will"?

_____
_____
_____
_____
_____
_____
_____
_____
_____
_____
_____
_____
_____
_____
_____
_____

Your Twisted Love

Your twisted love
Harms
brings sunshine to me
makes me want to cry
makes me happy
I wonder why

Your twisted love is
Painful
which makes it hurt
and then beautiful
to make it seem
Well Worth

Discussion Questions

1. What affects can longing for someone else's attention have on you?

_____
_____
_____
_____
_____
_____
_____

2. What makes us long for someone else's attention?

_____
_____
_____
_____
_____
_____
_____

3. Can you live happily with someone without them acknowledging you needs?

_____
_____
_____
_____
_____
_____
_____

4. Can you live happily with someone who is only concerned about their own needs?

_____
_____
_____
_____
_____
_____

I Long for Attention

I long for attention
the look, the glare, the smile
to let me know you love me
and make my body go wild

The same attention that you give
to others that you see
you turn and stare
forget I'm there
and don't consider me

I'll never understand
what kind of love is that
when you like to look at others
in front of my face
and behind my back

I long for a relationship
where I'm the only one
and all the special attention
Is given to me underneath the sun

I do not want from others
what I should get from you
I wish you understood me
or even had a clue

Love is much more than words
It comforts a lonely soul
and will carry your relationship
until we both grow old

Discussion Questions

1. Is there be a price for love? Explain.

_____
_____
_____
_____
_____
_____
_____
_____

2. Should there be a price for love? Explain.

_____
_____
_____
_____
_____
_____
_____
_____

3. How can you pay a price for love?

_____
_____
_____
_____
_____
_____
_____

4. Should people marry for money not love? Why or Why not?

_____
_____
_____
_____
_____
_____
_____

What's the Cost of Your Love?

What's the cost of your love
You said that it was free
What is the cost of your love
Is it just for me

What is the cost of your love
You said it was full of joy
But the cost of your love
You play just like a boy

What is the cost of your love
You said there was no other
What's the cost of your love
Don't treat me like another

What is the cost of your love
Do I have to deal with that
What's the cost of your love
I'm not and that's a fact

What's the cost of your love
You lay down with another
What's the cost of your love
Then you blame the other

What is the cost of your love
The price is much too high
Who would pay for that love
You're crazy and it's goodbye

Discussion Questions

1. What dynamic of a relationship is expressed in this poem?

_____

_____

_____

_____

_____

_____

_____

2. What causes a relationship to reflect the character expressed in this poem?

_____

_____

_____

_____

_____

_____

_____

3. Can a relationship, as expressed in the poem, be sustained as it is?

_____

_____

_____

_____

_____

_____

_____

4. What can be done to fix this type of relationship, If anything?

_____

_____

_____

_____

_____

_____

Trains Passing in the Night

We are like two trains
passing in the night
we see each other
but don't have time
to stop
explore the possibilities
to savor
the moment
to enjoy
what life has to offer us
we are on a mission
to nowhere
to somewhere
that is nowhere
we are like two
trains passing
in the night
we hear each other
but don't
communicate
we are on a schedule
to an imaginary life
full of ourselves
with only our lives
that matter and
focused on
going nowhere
together
alone
two trains passing by

Discussion Questions

1. Should there be roles for men and women in a relationship?

_____

_____

_____

_____

_____

_____

_____

_____

_____

2. Are there healthy roles for men and women in a relationship?

_____

_____

_____

_____

_____

_____

_____

_____

3. Should one person in the relationship create or designate the roles for the people in the relationship?

_____

_____

_____

_____

_____

_____

_____

_____

_____

Are You Waiting for Me Too...

Are you waiting for me too...

Buy your food
Fix your meals
Make your bed
Baby for real

Iron your shirts
Fill your tank
Be a maid
Let me be frank

Rub your back
Run your bath
Wash your clothes
Make your cash

As your equal
a working contributor
and your wife
you must be joking
get a life

Discussion Questions

1. Can love be conquered or does love happen naturally?

_____
_____
_____
_____
_____
_____
_____
_____
_____
_____

2. Do you think love need ever to be won or must it be given?

_____
_____
_____
_____
_____
_____
_____
_____
_____

3. If you have to win love, what is the best way to win someone's love?

_____
_____
_____
_____
_____
_____
_____
_____
_____

How Can I Conquer Your Love

How can I conquer your love
I don't believe it's true
Your love is transparent
and I don't know what to do

How can I conquer your love
It seems light years away
Your actions are so very clear
and they don't want me to stay

How can I conquer your love
I hurt so much inside
Your love's not real emotion
and I must get off this ride

How can I conquer your love
The pain I know is real
Your actions make my heart ache
You don't see how I feel

How can I conquer your love
I swear I can't go on
Your actions say you hate me
and baby now I'm gone

You don't love me I can see
Why don't you let me go
I can't continue to play this game
You make me feel so low

I hate this feeling now
The ache goes on and on
I hope that this is over soon
So I can begin a new love song

Discussion Questions

1. Is it possible to change a person?

_____

_____

_____

_____

_____

_____

_____

_____

_____

_____

_____

_____

_____

_____

2. Should you go into a relationship believing that you can change another person?

_____

_____

_____

_____

_____

_____

_____

_____

_____

_____

_____

_____

_____

How Can I Change You

How can I change you
I really tried my best
to live up to your expectations
and overcome your test

I can't live up to you
Nor change you if I try
Your demands are unreasonable
and I won't even tell a lie

You make me feel so blue
unless I bring more cash
I know that this is true
but you can kiss my ass

I believe if I had more money
I could do and be your honey
No matter bad or nice
with any kind of vice

I'd snap my fingers and
you'd come running by my side
The words and vows we've taken
are only for the ride

Your actions are determined
By my payment due each day
as long as I pay your bill
you never more will stray

Until you see another
Who listens to your lies
and gets caught in your dungeon
that's full of horror and cries

You've wooed other women
and say you love her too
and think that I'm the selfish one
because I won't share you

My love will never change you
Your price is just too grand
to reap the benefit of your love
is nothing I can stand

Suppressive Love

"You don't understand the power of giving and true love. You will never reap or feel magnificent love because of your suppressive love... the benefits of giving yourself to another." - Mary Love Dance

Discussion Questions

1. Why would a person have feeling those expressed in the poem?

_____
_____
_____
_____
_____
_____
_____
_____
_____
_____

2. Is it hard for love to grow?

_____
_____
_____
_____
_____
_____
_____
_____
_____

3. Should it be hard for love to grow?

_____
_____
_____
_____
_____
_____
_____
_____
_____

Love

Love
Love
Love
Love
Wait
Is there Love
Or is there Hate
Love
Yes
No
Love
No
No
There is no love
For you to show
Love
Love
Love
It's shining bright
Love
Love
Love
It's like the night
Love
Love
No
No
No
No
No
No
Love
No
Love
Why wont it Grow

Discussion Questions

1. Why is love a flower in this poem?

_____

_____

_____

_____

_____

_____

_____

_____

_____

_____

_____

_____

_____

_____

2. Can you relate love to another metaphor (object or thing)?
Abuse in a relationship should never be tolerated. If you think you are
being abused, call an abuse hotline 800-799-7233.

_____

_____

_____

_____

_____

_____

_____

_____

_____

_____

_____

_____

_____

_____

Your Love is Like a Flower

Your love is like a flower
that opens with the sun
So beautiful
So bright
So enjoyable
To everyone
And then the darkness
falls
upon you
and you close
you become something new
a different person I suppose

Your love is like a flower
you draw me in so close
your smile
your look
your hand
your hook
You draw me in so close

But when the darkness falls
Your love closes just like a flower
and I don't know
which way to go
or what's the coming hour

Your love is like a flower
So beautiful and bright
It pulls me in
I'm scared again
afraid I have to fight

I want to go
I'm scared to leave
cause I'm use to having you
I want to stay or runaway
I'm searching for a clue

When You Love Someone

When you love someone
will you sulk and cry
When you have your shortcoming
blame them or say goodbye

Do you understand the price
that you're about to pay
Can you really give it up
each and every day

Love is so complicated
or so that's what they say
And if you love someone
you may wish for another day

If it's about you and you alone
then baby you should go
Cause if you love somebody right
It's so much more you know

True love endures your hardships
and understands your pain
It doesn't look for an easy escape
with temporary gains

For life will challenge your love
and make you want to cry
But what you have to understand
is love will never die

So if you truly love someone
there's nothing you won't do
To honor your vows
and with God's help
till death due part you two

So check yourself
and watch your step
before you walk the line
Cause the journey
You're about to take
It's till the end of time

Discussion Questions

1. Is love hard? Explain?

_____

_____

_____

2. Why is easier to blame someone you love rather than accept
responsibility yourself?

_____

_____

_____

3. How can love make you want to cry?

_____

_____

_____

4. Do you understand the magnitude of the marriage vows?

_____

_____

_____

You Live and Hope to Find

You live and hope to find
someone who has your hopes and dreams in mind
but life is not always what it seems
and what you think you have will complicate your dreams

So you live to witness time
and sometimes want to scream
because you realize "You" have to shine
To bring about your Dreams
You can't depend on anyone else
to see the world like you
Even though the fairytale life
it seems that couples do
Together we can have our dreams
only when you believe in me and I believe in you

But when you have no focus, desire and drive
your dreams will surely pass you by
While you sit and wonder why
You are waiting for a collective goal
That will die before you both grow old

Cause what you don't realize
is that your dreams and goals
don't have the foundation, support or love
it takes for them to unfold

So all you can do is do it yourself
When no one's on your side
and one of you doesn't believe or care
to see it materialize

Discussion Questions

1. Do you think a relationship mirrors a business relationship?

_____

_____

_____

_____

_____

_____

2. What role can support from your spouse play in the achievement of your dreams?

_____

_____

_____

_____

_____

_____

3. Are you capable of making your dreams materialize by yourself?

_____

_____

_____

_____

_____

_____

4. Is it easy for you to give love to people you don't know?

_____

_____

_____

_____

_____

_____

5. How can you improve your kindness to make the world a better place?

_____

_____

_____

_____

Just One Day

If God gives you love for just one day
How much would you be able to give away
or would your life get in the way
and would you save it for another day

If God told you to use it now
Would you have problems understanding how
to give your love to all you see
and help them become the best they can be

If God told you don't you wait
until you get to the pearly gate
Would you say God it's not up to me
to give out love so freely

If God told you it's up to you
to find a way and break through
Would you listen, try and love
Someone today not from above
Or would you sit and make delay
and waste your precious time away

Love is free the more you give
the more you really want to live
It brings you gifts you never see
and makes you what you're meant to be
So don't you wait for special signs
or dreams or orders from the divine

Make it your mission today
and don't delay
or wait for a perfect day
The more you give
The more you'll see
That love is best when given free

Discussion Question

1. Discuss the beauty of love and how it can be transmitted by a single look or touch.

_____
_____
_____
_____
_____
_____
_____
_____
_____
_____
_____
_____
_____
_____
_____
_____
_____
_____
_____
_____
_____
_____
_____
_____
_____
_____
_____
_____
_____
_____
_____
_____
_____
_____

Look at Me

When you look at me
I can
feel
your love

When you look at me
I can
see
it's from above

When you look at me
I can
smile
within

When you look at me
I can
say
Amen

Discussion Questions

1. Are words enough to make you fall in love?

_____
_____
_____
_____
_____
_____
_____
_____
_____
_____
_____
_____
_____
_____
_____
_____
_____
_____
_____

2. What else can you do assure another person that you love them?

_____
_____
_____
_____
_____
_____
_____
_____
_____
_____
_____
_____
_____
_____
_____
_____
_____
_____

Falling

You whisper sweetly in my ear
The words you know I want to hear
I love you
I need you
You're beautiful
You're the queen of my life

You whisper calmly in my ear
You never ever need to fear
me straying
me playing
mc desiring
anyone but you

You whisper patiently in my ear
and tell me softly you will always be near
I can't live without you
or will ever doubt you
I'm yours
I'm falling
I'm in love with you

Discussion Questions

1. Do you believe that love should have a price?

_____

_____

_____

_____

_____

_____

_____

_____

_____

2. Is love real if it is given in vain or because of what you want from someone else?

_____

_____

_____

_____

_____

_____

_____

_____

_____

3. Do you ever wonder about love that is based on what you do for the person.
If you could no longer give to them would they still love you?

_____

_____

_____

_____

_____

_____

_____

_____

The Cost of Your Love

The cost of your love
is way too high
If I could even touch the sky
I would not be able to
reach your heights
or understand
or pay the price
to have the love
that you can give
or pay the price
or even live
up to your standards
there is no way
for any human to pay today

The cost of your love
is way to vast
If I reach the depths of the sea
It could not pay that crazy fee
or comprehend
your type of love
or be worthy
is it from above?
No! cause it's not real love
this is a debt
I can't pay
it's not for me
and never meant
to rock my world
it's one of a kind
and it will surely
never be mine!

Hate

"I don't love your hate but I do hate your love"

"Love doesn't give you the right to treat me wrong, love doesn't give you the right to lie, love doesn't give you the right to disrespect me, love doesn't give you the right." - Mary Love Dance

Discussion Questions

1. Can the passion of true love produce hate? Explain.

_____

_____

_____

_____

_____

_____

_____

_____

_____

_____

_____

_____

_____

_____

_____

_____

2. Is it true that there a thin line between love and hate? Explain.

_____

_____

_____

_____

_____

_____

_____

_____

_____

_____

_____

_____

_____

_____

_____

I Hate You

I hate you
Oh, no that's a lie
I hate you
Then I'll say good bye

I hate you
I really love you so
I hate you
Should I really go

I hate you
I love you more each day
I hate you
I think I'm gonna pray

I hate you
You don't deserve my heart
I hate you
Divine from the start

I hate you
My tears are flowing fast
I hate you
I think I'm going to crash

I hate you
I don't know what to do
I hate you
I think that we are through

I hate you
I'll escape this pain tonight
I hate you
It makes me want to fight

and now my future's bright

Goodbye

Hate is on Your Shoulders

Hate is on your shoulders
It's hard for you to see
That your each and every action
is meant to get at me

Hate is on your head
It occupies your brain
That all your movements indicate
It's driving you insane

Hate is on your back
You give it constantly
It's creeping up and down your spine
You're throwing it at me

Hate is in your veins
It flows through you each day
You spew it out like words of love
and never to delay

Hate is in your heart
It beats just like a drum
You hate so much you don't realize
From which way it will come

Hate is in your eyes
It cuts through like a knife
And you don't care whose in despair
You want to take their life

Hate has overcome you
You've got to let it go
The devil's in your soul again
And you don't even know

Why do you hate what you do not see
The harm that you create
The funny thing is that you think
You'll enter the pearly gate

Discussion Questions

1. How is hate manifested in people?

_____

_____

2. What causes a person to hate?

_____

_____

3. Does hate have anything to do with how a person is raised or is hate a byproduct of one's environment?

_____

_____

I Hear You Cry

I hear you cry
Your smile belies the grief you bear
It's written in your eyes
You play the game of the world
but I still see your pain
It's hard to be so strong and brave
Amidst the loss and gains
And you sit and wonder why
You feel it worth the fame

It's my life you say and this is true
I'm sad because of your grief
It causes you to linger in sadness
and this gives you no peace
So open up your eyes
and know, that God has a special plan for you
You don't have to stoop so low
like other people do

For The Love of Money
Fame and Fortune
It robs you of your soul
You reap the benefits now
But hell will be your goal
So break the cycle, let it go...
For you know that it is said
That all things are possible
Because Jesus died and bled

Discussion Questions

1. Have you ever met someone and immediately felt his or her pain?

_____

_____

_____

_____

2. Have you helped someone change his or her attitude?

_____

_____

_____

_____

3. What are some things that can rob you of your soul?

_____

_____

_____

_____

4. Is love selfish, rude and crude?

_____

_____

_____

_____

5. Does love envy, cause pain or drive you insane?

_____

_____

_____

_____

6. Why would love be about gain?

_____

_____

_____

_____

Why I Hate Your Love

I hate your love because
It's selfish
It's rude
It's mindless
It's crude

It envies
It's pain
It's crazy
It's driving me insane

It's self-centered
It blames
It's awful
It's full of games

I hate your love because
It's familiar
and It's all about gain

Discussion Questions

1. What does seduction mean to you?

_____
_____
_____
_____
_____
_____
_____
_____
_____
_____

2. Do you believe that being seduces is important in a loving relationship?

_____
_____
_____
_____
_____
_____
_____
_____
_____
_____

3. Can seduction improve your relationship?

_____
_____
_____
_____
_____
_____
_____
_____
_____

Seductive Love

"Seduction can be beautiful when desired by two and can be a hazard if desired by one." - Mary Love Dance

Discussion Questions

1. Is the phrase "I Love You" enough to sustain a relationship?

_____

_____

_____

_____

_____

_____

_____

_____

_____

_____

_____

_____

_____

_____

_____

2. How can couples build a strong relationship grounded on love?

_____

_____

_____

_____

_____

_____

_____

_____

_____

_____

_____

_____

_____

_____

When You Say You Love Me

When you say
you love me
Do you understand
what that entails
It's so much deeper
and most certainly grand
In other words
It's patience
when I make you mad
It's forgiveness
when I make you sad
It's sacrifice
when you don't really care
It's forgiveness
when no one is there
It's giving
when you want to say no
It's consideration
when you want to go
It's not envy
when I excel
It's togetherness
that makes us prevail.

Discussion Question

1. Does love come before passion or does passion come before love? Explain.

_____
_____
_____
_____
_____
_____
_____
_____
_____
_____
_____
_____
_____
_____
_____
_____
_____
_____
_____
_____
_____
_____
_____
_____
_____
_____
_____
_____
_____
_____
_____
_____

Passion

Passion
burns
in my heart
the fire
burns
on my lips
I shiver
sparks fly
my desires
oh how
you
light
my
fire

Discussion Questions

1. What makes a person feel special in a relationship?

_____

_____

_____

_____

_____

_____

_____

_____

_____

_____

2. Should what makes you feel good be discussed before marriage?

_____

_____

_____

_____

_____

_____

_____

_____

_____

3. How can communicating your needs help a relationship?

_____

_____

_____

_____

_____

_____

_____

_____

_____

_____

Your Queen

I long to be your queen
The one you hold so near

The one that you admire
Your one and only dear

I want to be your queen
The one right by your side

You'll be my king
There's nothing for me to hide

If I become your queen
Our lives will be much better

I will serve your every need
and deliver to you whatever

If you make me your queen
our happiness will begin

And our true transformation
Will cause our lives to hinge

Discussion Questions

1. Who do you go to for advice on love?

_____

_____

_____

_____

_____

_____

2. How does fun play into the longevity of a relationship?

_____

_____

_____

_____

_____

_____

3. Should you look for someone who has interest similar to yours? Explain.

_____

_____

_____

_____

_____

_____

4. Do opposites attract?

_____

_____

_____

_____

_____

_____

My Love is Exponential

My love is exponential
A zillion going strong
For me it is so simple
and nothing can go wrong

My love is extra ordinary
Beyond the moon and back
I'll be right here forever
and you can depend on that

My love is consequential
and you will see that it's true
and understand how much I care
Because I'll give it all to you

My love grows enormously
each and every day
The excitement is contagious
and it won't ever decay

My love is designed for you
Our souls have become one
So buckle up and enjoy the ride
get ready for some fun

Discussion Questions

1. When love takes hold of you does it become magical when and only when you feel the feeling too?

_____

_____

_____

_____

_____

_____

_____

_____

2. If someone loves you and you don't have the some feeling for him or her is that a good reason to not explore the relationship?

_____

_____

_____

_____

_____

_____

_____

_____

3. When you love someone do you truly put his or her needs and wants before yours?

_____

_____

_____

_____

_____

_____

_____

_____

When Love Takes Hold of You

When love takes hold of you
There's nothing you can do
You think that you can hide
and let your feeling slide

More powerful than the wind
and unexpected like the rain
It comes and it will pin
you underneath it's pain

It's as intense as any star
and faster then your car
The light will shine so bright
and overcome your might

When love takes hold of you
Your life for sure will change
For you put others needs and wants
Before you and your gains

Discussion Questions

1. What circumstances and scenarios can break a relationship?

_____

_____

_____

_____

_____

_____

_____

2. How can thinking only of yourself hurt a relationship?

_____

_____

_____

_____

_____

_____

_____

3. How can you guard against letting the world breakup your relationship?

_____

_____

_____

_____

_____

_____

_____

4. What kind of person breaks up relationships?

_____

_____

_____

_____

_____

_____

The One Has Become Two

The one has become two
There's nothing more to do
I know this kind of love
is not from heaven above

The one has become two
it seems unfair but true
The road to two seems grand
but you don't understand

The one has become two
The vows have gone away
and never really stayed
from your wedding day

The one has become two
Why do you continue through
and cause each other pain
because this is so lame

The one has become two
and baby you are through
So say your last good byes
And save your tears and cries

The one has become two

Discussion Questions

1. Do you think people marry to impress others?

_____

_____

_____

_____

_____

_____

_____

2. What factors besides love play a part in marriage selection?

_____

_____

_____

_____

_____

_____

_____

3. Is there anything wrong with factors other than love impacting a marriage decision? Explain.

_____

_____

_____

_____

_____

_____

_____

4. Is marriage ever a game? Discuss.

_____

_____

_____

_____

_____

_____

_____

Convenient Love

You married me out of convenience
It really was a show
To prove to those around you
That you could make it so
You never truly loved me
You got me now you go
The conquest is completed
and this much I do know

You married me for greed
A beauty on your arm
To shows your boys you got me
That I could be your charm
There's no way for you
To deny my claim you see
Because when it comes to loving me
We never will agree

The way you feel about me
is one big fat stupid lie
You're out to please yourself
and show that you're the "guy"
To manipulate and trick
Someone and break their heart
You don't care how you make me feel
and you knew it from the start

Discussion Questions

1. Have you had a magical (euphoric) feeling with someone you love?

_____

_____

_____

_____

_____

_____

_____

_____

_____

_____

_____

_____

_____

_____

_____

_____

2. How can you keep the euphoric feeling in your relationship?

_____

_____

_____

_____

_____

_____

_____

_____

_____

_____

_____

_____

_____

_____

_____

I feel Something

With you I feel something
It's magical and true

You look at me and instinctively
you know just what to do

You understand and read my heart
it's like your open book

You light my fire and take me higher
and I believe I'm hooked

There's no illusion in your world
my life it feels complete

There's nothing here to bring me fear
or make me feel defeat

You care for me like no other
You understand God's plan

And you take into consideration
Our love is vast and grand

Discussion Question

1. Do you believe in soul-mates? Explain why or why not.

_____
_____
_____
_____
_____
_____
_____
_____
_____
_____
_____
_____
_____
_____
_____
_____
_____
_____
_____
_____
_____
_____
_____
_____
_____
_____
_____
_____
_____
_____
_____
_____

My Spirit is Touched

How can I describe this feeling
that I have inside
Some say you have a soul-mate
It's blowing up my mind

My Spirit was touched today
my soul is yearning for you now
Your voice it makes me smile
and I want to be with you some how

This dilemma I'm experiencing
is certainly off the chain
it will knock you off your feet
and complicates your game

No consummation happened
the love is in our hearts
we feel that this happened
and we must now depart

Were you really made for me
Then why are you with another
and trying to play the game of love
seemingly undercover

Why do you think it is ok
You think that you are smart
That we could be together
You are playing with my heart

I will not let this sinful lust
Corrupt my heart and soul
You need to take control of your body
Cause baby it's made of gold

So don't allow your body
To control what you should do
Use your brain and always maintain
Your dignity through and through

Morning, Noon or Night

It's early in the morning
and I'm thinking of you
I pray to the Lord
What should I do
I know that this feeling is wrong
but you make me feel so right
I must control myself
So this feeling doesn't take flight

It's in the afternoon
I'm thinking of you again
I want to call to hear your voice
but trying to pretend
that I don't want you
and never will give my love
to sin and fornicate
and disrespect the Lord above

It's late at night
my soul is taking flight
My body is still yearning for you
to lay next to you
but that will never
come true
why do I long for you

Discussion Questions

1. What causes love to wonder?

_____

_____

_____

2. How can a relationship grow, develop and improve love throughout the years?

_____

_____

_____

3. Can communication help a relationship grow? Explain

_____

_____

_____

4. From the outside looking in, many relationships seem better than they are. How can you use outside impressions to improve your relationship?

_____

_____

_____

5. Is it true that you get what you ask for, otherwise you would be married to someone else?

_____

_____

_____

6. Do you see the good in your mate or do you find yourself focusing on their faults?

_____

_____

_____

7. How can you make the relationship you have work?

_____

_____

_____

A Touch Unknown Seems

A touch unknown seems grand
but is it all that you planned
your perception and reality
may never meet
and you realize and see
that what you're imagining
what could not be
and is as far as
the ocean is deep

Because you wish that it might be
doesn't mean that it will

A touch untouched
and only imagined
is only a figment of your imagination
fiction
you know
in your brain
playing games

A movie on the screen
you want it to come true
but the reality is
it may never
come to fruition for you
oh, the pain that it gives your heart
that we truly
Will probably always be apart

Discussion Questions

1. What have you learned from this book?

_____

_____

_____

_____

_____

2. How can you use the positive in your relationship to grow your love?

_____

_____

_____

_____

_____

3. Why is it important to seek advice from couples who have relationships you admire?

_____

_____

_____

_____

_____

4. Do you believe that what's good for one couple/relationship may not be good for another couple/relationship?

_____

_____

_____

_____

_____

5. Analyze all advice, pray and talk out what works for the relationship as a whole.

_____

_____

_____

_____

Make a list of all the reasons you think your partner fell in love with you. Share them with your partner and see if they agree with your list.

1.
2.
3.
4.
5.
6.
7.
8.
9.
10

Make a list of all the reason you fell in love with your partner. Let your partner know what made you fall in love with them.

1.
2.
3.
4.
5.
6.
7.
8.
9.
10.

Printed in the United States
by Baker & Taylor Publisher Services